ARReSTeD DeVeLOPMeNT™

And That's Why...
You Always Leave a Note.

RUNNING PRESS

PHILADELPHIA · LONDON

Books published by Running Press are available at special discounts for bulk purchases
in the United States by corporations, institutions, and other organizations. For more
information, please contact the Special Markets Department at the Perseus Books Group,
2300 Chestnut Street, Suite 200, Philadelphia, PA 19103, or call (800) 810-4145,
ext. 5000, or e-mail special.markets@perseusbooks.com.

ISBN 978-0-7624-5255-2
Library of Congress Control Number: 2013948618

E-book ISBN 978-0-7624-5318-4

9   8   7   6   5   4   3   2   1
Digit on the right indicates the number of this printing

Edited by Jennifer Leczkowski
Typography: Antique Olive and Blur

Running Press Book Publishers
2300 Chestnut Street
Philadelphia, PA 19103-4371

Visit us on the web!
www.runningpress.com

Contents

Introduction 4

Family First 6

Huge Mistakes 22

(Mis)Communication 38

Parental Guidance 54

Sink or Swim 70

Marry Me! 86

Hey, Brother 102

Risky Business 116

Growing Up 130

Introduction

WHEN family patriarch George Sr. is imprisoned for his shifty accounting practices, the Bluth family is forced to face reality—or not. With the family assets frozen and the family business in jeopardy, it looks like the Bluths will have to give up their lavish lifestyle.

The Bluths may live in a model home, but they're not exactly a model family. This dysfunctional bunch lie to each other, get into fistfights, take advantage of each other, and call each other names. But through it all, they stick together.

Sure, they've made some huge mistakes. From getting married on a dare, to some, um, light treason. But they've also learned some valuable life lessons. Like the importance of leaving a note. And putting family first. And watching out for hop-ons (you're gonna get some hop-ons).

On the following pages, we'll revisit some of the ups and downs of the Bluth family, and perhaps learn a few lessons about life, love, family, and *illusions*. After all, they said some wonderful things.

Family First

MICHAEL:

What comes before anything?
What have we always
said is the most important thing?

GEORGE MICHAEL:

Breakfast.

MICHAEL:

Family.

GEORGE MICHAEL:

Family, right. I thought
you meant of the things you eat.

I need a **favor.**

We ought to
put that on our **MICHAEL**
family crest.

MICHAEL:

I'm gonna go fishing with my
son here. We're gonna go
have some fun. Real fun. Okay?
Not everything is strippers and booze
and buckets of blood.

G.O.B.

Nobody
makes a fool
of our family
without
my help.

MAEBY

Ever get the feeling like you don't even matter?

Only when I'm around my children.

LUCILLE

LUCILLE:

Buster, what are you
doing with Mother's rape horn?
I have a rape horn, Michael, because
you took away my mace.

BUSTER:

Yeah, like anyone would
want to "R" her.

MICHAEL

Has anyone in this family ever even seen a chicken?

LINDSAY:

Did you enjoy your meal, Mom?
You drank it fast enough.

LUCILLE:

Not as much as you
enjoyed yours. You want your belt
to buckle, not your chair.

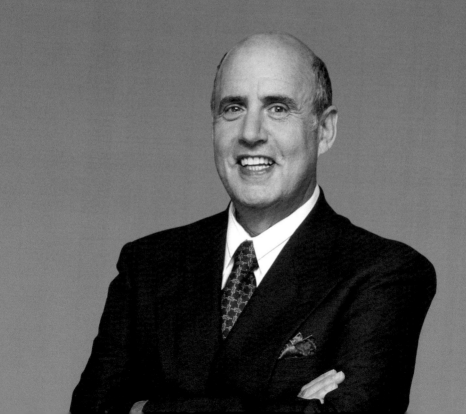

GEORGE SR.

There's a good chance
that I—

that I may
have committed
some, um,
light treason.

G.O.B.

Well, she was a darer.
She's one of those girls
who just dares you
to do things.

MICHAEL

You married her?

I needed a dare!

G.O.B.

24

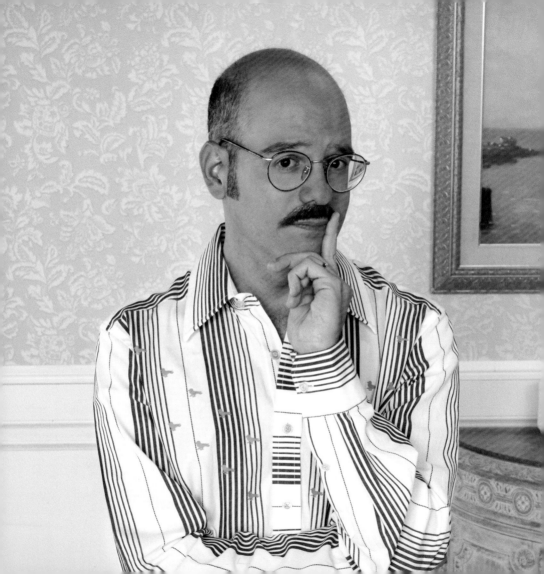

TOBIAS:

Well, yes, I'm afraid I
prematurely shot my wad, or what
was supposed to be a dry run,
if you will. So now I'm afraid I have
something of a mess
on my hands.

MICHAEL:

It's just—there's just so many poorly
chosen words in that sentence.

I've made a huge mistake.

GUARD

NO TOUCHING!

MICHAEL:
You're either going
to jail, or if the judge
shows absolutely no mercy at all,
you'll be staying
here with my mother.

You lied to me.
You said my father
was my father,
but my uncle is my father.

My father
is my uncle!

GEORGE SR.:

They're gonna kill Grandpa.
I gotta get out of here.
I'm an innocent man.
You gotta help Pop-pop get outta
here. Give me your hair.

GEORGE MICHAEL:

My hair?

GEORGE SR.:

Give me your hair.
Give Pop-pop your hair.

(Mis)Communication

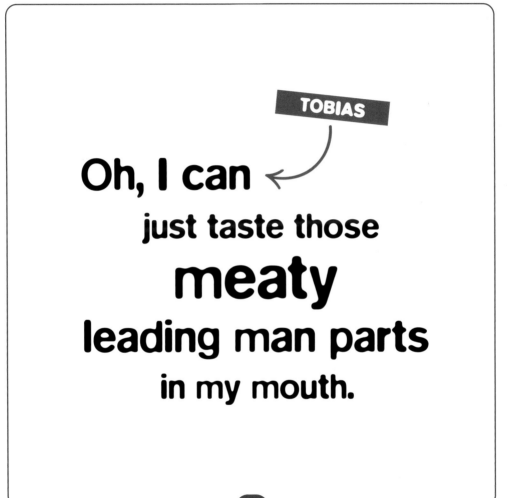

MAEBY:

Do you guys know
where I could get one of those gold
necklaces with the "t" on it?

MICHAEL:

That's a cross.

MAEBY:

Across from where?

I don't understand
the question,
and I won't
respond to it.

TOBIAS

I'm afraid I just
blue myself.

MICHAEL

There's gotta be
a better way to say that.

What's Spanish for "I know you speak English"?

It's as **Ann**
as the nose
on
plain's face.

MICHAEL

She's a little bit more like me. It's like we finish each other's—

LINDSAY

Sandwiches?

MRS. FEATHERBOTTOM:
Who'd like "a banger in the mouth"?
Oh! Right! I forgot. Here in
the states, you call it
"a sausage in the mouth."

MICHAEL:
We just call it "sausage."

Parental Guidance

LUCILLE:
I don't have the milk of mother's kindness in me anymore.

MICHAEL:
Yeah, that udder's been dry for a while now, hasn't it?

MICHAEL:

She's always got to wedge herself in the middle of us so she can control everything.

BUSTER:

Yeah. Mom's awesome. Maybe we should call her.

LUCILLE

Oh, she thinks

I'm too critical.

That's another fault

of hers.

G.O.B.

Moms ← are such a pain in the ass, huh?

It's like "Die already!"

I'm looking for **something** that says,

TOBIAS

"Dad likes **leather.**"

That's all I ever wanted from you,

Daddy.

For you to spend money on me.

LUCILLE:

Now that your father
has deserted us, Buster's
become impossible to control.
Suddenly he's too much
of a big shot to
brush Mother's hair.

LINDSAY:

You need to learn a
little discipline.

MAEBY:

Hmm. Nope, that doesn't
feel right.

LINDSAY:

No, no, no. I'm telling you.
You are now punished.
I punish thee.

Sink or Swim

It's called **taking advantage.**

G.O.B.

It's what gets you ahead in life.

GEORGE SR.:
I haven't had a vacation
in years. This is my vacation.
I'm exercising. I'm sleeping well.

MICHAEL:
You're doing time.

GEORGE SR.:
I'm doing the time of my life.

VISITORS
EVERY PERSON WHO BREAKS DOW
ANY JAIL, OR ANY PUBLIC PROPER
PROSECUTION, CONVICTION IS
ND BY IMPRISONMENT IN
RSONA QUE QUEBRE, A
UALQUIER PROPIEDAD P
DO, CONVICCIÓN ES CAST
SERA ENCARCELADO EN L

TOBIAS

I'll be your wingman.
Even if it means
me taking a
chubby,
I will suck it up.

MICHAEL:
I mean, if you'd tried
and failed, I'd understand, but
you didn't even try.

LINDSAY:
So, I didn't even fail,
and I don't see you giving
me credit for that.

GEORGE SR.:

I'm under a lot of pressure.
I'm trying to get my newsletter off
the ground, and I'm trying
to decide which gang to align
myself with.

LUCILLE

Michael, what are
you doing tomorrow?

MICHAEL

Having my day ruined with
whatever you're about to
ask me to do.

G.O.B.:

I'm a complete failure.

GEORGE SR.:

Where'd you
get that kind of talk?

G.O.B.:

From you. You always
say that about me.

BUSTER:

They're taking me in the army. They didn't think there was enough wrong with me.

LUCILLE:

Well, did they check everything?

BUSTER:

Yes, they even touched my Charlie Browns.

Marry Me!

LINDSAY:

My husband dumped me and ran
off to Vegas with Kitty.
That bleached blonde whore.

MICHAEL:

He's definitely got a type.

GEORGE MICHAEL

She's kind of
my girlfriend.

MICHAEL

Her?

LUCILLE:

What, did that Mexican
throw you out?

G.O.B.:

She's not "that Mexican,"
Mom. She's my Mexican. And she's
Colombian or something.

GEORGE SR.

Daddy horny, Michael.

MICHAEL:

Maybe it's time you got out
there and started meeting
people, you know, meeting women.
Meeting women who didn't
give birth to you.

If I look like a man
who made love
to his wife last night,

it's because
I almost did.

TOBIAS

BUSTER:

That's what you do when
life hands you a chance to be with
someone special. You just grab
that—that brownish
area by its points, and you
don't let go no matter what your
mom says.

I've got the marriage
and none of the good parts.
It's like so far it's been

all chain
and no ball.

MICHAEL

So this is the magic trick, huh?

G.O.B.

Illusion, Michael.
A trick is something
a whore does for money.

Or candy.

LINDSAY:
Michael, if this is a lecture
on how we're all
supposed to whatever
and blah, blah, blah, well, you can
save it, 'cause we all
know it by heart.

I don't see
you crying,
robot!

You taste these tears.
Taste my sad, Michael.

MICHAEL:

I've got a nice, hard cot
with his name on it.

LUCILLE:

You'd do that to your own brother?

MICHAEL:

I said "cot."

Hit me in the face!
Hit me in the face!
Hit me in the face!

BUSTER

MICHAEL:
You've got to be the laziest
person in the world.

LINDSAY:
If you weren't all the
way on the other side of the room,
I'd slap your face.

Risky Business

GEORGE MICHAEL:
Yeah, but if I fail math,
there goes my chance at a good job
and a happy life of hard work,
like you always say.

TOBIAS

Are you forgetting that I was a professional twice over?

An analyst and a therapist.

The world's first "analrapist."

Come on, you douche bags. We're all on the same team!

BUSTER

There's always **GEORGE SR.** money in the banana stand.

MICHAEL:
I'm gonna give you a promotion.
Welcome aboard, Mr. Manager.

GEORGE MICHAEL:
Wow, I'm Mr. Manager!

MICHAEL:
Well, manager. We just say
"manager."

My brother wasn't
optimistic it could be done.

But I didn't take
"wasn't optimistic
it could be done"
for an answer.

G.O.B.:

Hey, I'm the President now.
Filling Dad's shoes literally, except
his shoes don't fit. But I did
finally get into Dad's pants,
although I had to have the crotch
taken in a little.

Growing Up

MAEBY:

I don't care, and I'm not
saying "I don't care" like kids who say
they don't care when they
really do care—
'cause I really don't care.

BUSTER:

I mean, there is so much
in life that I have not experienced.
And now that I'm away from Mom,
I feel like this is my chance to live.
I want to dance. I want to make love
to a woman. I want to get a
checking account.

GEORGE MICHAEL

Yeah, I'm gonna need
a leather jacket

for when I'm on my hog
and need to go
into a controlled slide.

BUSTER

Wow, we're just blowing through naptime, aren't we?

You've never even
thrown a ball
around with me.

Great. Now you're
an athlete.

BUSTER:

I decided to sleep in the car
so my snoring wouldn't
bother you, and I left that
recording of my snoring so you
wouldn't know I'm gone.

Ah, le clumsy adolescence.
It's a phase we've all been through.
Except for me.
I was like a cat.

I always ended up
on all fours.

Like a cat.